For all beings in the world:

May you always remember

WHO YOU TRULY ARE

And that

YOU ARE WHOLE

And as you journey through life

Remember

YOU ARE
THE AUTHOR
OF
YOUR LIFE

This Guide Book is designed for you and your inner child to create a unique experience as you draw, read, write, reflect and explore all the ways you can reconnect to your wholeness and live a passionate and authentic life. I've used metaphors of earth, tree and leaves to help facilitate the journey.

The psychological and scientific foundations of this book come from: Eco-psychology, Neuroscience, Environmental Stewardship, Somatics and Resilience, Meditation and Mindfulness, Positive Psychology, Non-Violent Communication and the Hoffman Quadrinity Process.

Included are visioning, reading, writing, poetry, songs and more. Each is designed to affirm your unique gifts, help you honor your body, heart and mind so you can find strength and balance while you stay connected to your inner wisdom and expand your resilience as you journey through life.

By reading and completing the exercises you will learn valuable skills that will support your life's journey and healing: validation, resilience, forgiveness, compassion, gratitude, health and wellness, naming and accepting feelings and sensations, releasing feelings, boundary setting, centering, visioning, honoring your wholeness and the wholeness of others.

The gift of claiming who you truly are awaits you as you learn to ground in the strength of your uniqueness, follow your inner guidance and live whole. This book is about your body, emotional self, intellect and Spirit claiming your essence and allowing yourself to dream, to be present, have passion and shine your unique light in the world!

As Mark Twain put is so eloquently, "The two most important days are the day you were born and the day you find out why."

Living Whole is a colorful inner journey to discover and commit to sharing your unique contribution that only you can give to the world!

~ Linda

**Luna Madre™ Publishing**
3463 State Street, Suite 225
Santa Barbara CA 93105
www.LunaMadre.com



Printed in the United States. Luna Madre Publishing.
**www.GrowingUpWhole.com**

**Living Whole™ A Guide Book**

ISBN: 978-0-9962065-0-1
Editor: Annie J. Dahlgren
Illustrations: Linda Newlin
Graphics Cover: Cecilia Martini Muth, CC Design, Santa Barbara

# This is your Guide Book

A Guide Book to awaken and expand your awareness and validate your uniqueness so you can live the life you came here to live and give your unique gifts and talents.

It is a journey through experiences, writing, reading, artwork, songs and adventures designed to enhance your life skills to support you on your life's journey.

You can write or draw if you are moved to express yourself creatively and thus make it your own unique experience within the explorations and practices presented here.

I heard a story about a young man who went to a spiritual teacher to ask this question:

"Why does it say in the Teachings,
Keep the words ON your heart?
and not
IN your heart?"

The teacher says, "That is an excellent question young man.

The answer is...

Until one allows their heart to open the words can not fall in."

I invite you to open your heart
and allow the words
that you find within your self
to fall in

so they can strengthen
and direct you
on your unique life's journey.

You will then be able to decide what to
let into your heart,
your mind, your body and your space.

Finding your voice, your purpose and your
capacity to say YES
to what is in your highest good.

The world needs you to

Be The One and Only YOU

and the greatest hope is that

You will always Shine
Your Unique Light

Through all the seasons
of your life.

# When were you born?

---

This is the miraculous day of your birth! Oh Happy Day ☺!

# Where on the earth were you born?

---

What season was it?

Where do you live now?

List your favorite things about where you live now:

You

are part of

the

Earth's Energy

Scientists have discovered that our bodies contain molecules from the stars.

STAR DUST IS INSIDE YOU.

What do you think about this?

What would you change about how you treat your body?

Imagine the stardust inside of you.
What does it feel like?

Tonight go look at the stars and
notice how it feels to look at them.

# We Need the Earth

We need the AIR to breathe

We need the RAIN to grow all living things

We need the EARTH to sustain us

We need the SUN to give us light

## EXERCISE:

Go outside or sit where you can see the sun and be in its rays.

Breathe in the sun's light and feel the warmth within you.

Take time to experience the peace and strength that the sun offers to you.

Feel the energy of the sun inside your body and let the good feelings run through all of you.

Name the sensations/feelings that you feel here in the sun:

We grow like trees grow, in rich soil with:

Circle the ones that YOU NEED

to grow and be strong:

Clean Air Water Sun

Kindness Joy Laughter

Love Support Peace

Friends Family Time to Have Fun

Nourishing Food Safety Rest

Purpose Pleasure Community

# The Earth is My Home

## Exercise:

Go outside in nature.

Let your self walk around and find a favorite spot.

Become still and listen.

What do you hear, smell, see?

What do you notice happening inside you when you're connecting with the earth?

Circle the ones that describe how you experience the earth to be:

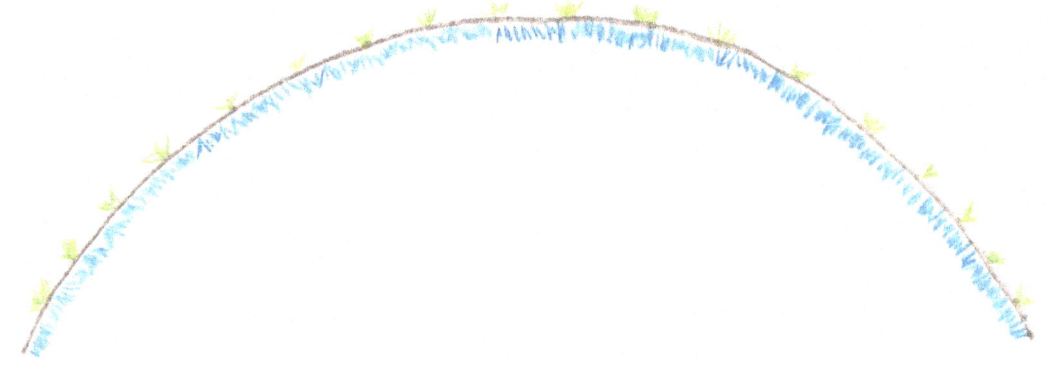

Life giving Peaceful Green

Soft Kind Strong

Grounded Warm Safe Windy

Wet Dry Hot Amazing

BIG Colorful Beautiful Fun

Breezy Magical Mysterious

# The Earth Needs Us

The earth is a living being just like you are.

What are some things you can do to help keep the earth strong and healthy?

(some things people are doing around the world include: recycling, picking up trash, not using paper products, riding their bikes, walking, planting trees and conserving water).

Your Body
Is the Home
of
Your Spirit ♡

# My Body is the Home of My Spirit♡

I help my body to stay
healthy and strong

by giving it nutritious food
fun/play and rest

stretching and meditation
sleep and water

loving kindness and friendship
gratitude and sunlight

## Circle the things you feed your body:

Vegetables Water Fresh Fruit

Meat Fish Eggs Dairy

Soy Nuts Seeds

Grains Green Drinks Vitamins

## Other things I do to be healthy:

Circle the Ones that You Do:

Run Play team sports Stretch

Ride Horses Gymnastics Ski Swim

Hike Weights Rock Climbing Learn

Bicycling Walk/Run My Dog Sleep

Yoga Meditate Brush/Floss Dance

Vitamins Rest Be With Friends/Family

Tennis Cricket Rugby No Smoking

Avoid drugs Limit Alcohol Drive safely

## My body grows each year like a tree.

If I were a tree, this is the kind of tree I would be.

Draw, paint or sketch it here:

---

We need

Sun Light

to Grow

A five year old told this story to his classmates about

## The Big Bang Theory

"Once upon a time there was the SUN.

One day there was a big bang
and the sun exploded
into millions of pieces.

That is how the Light
got into
each and every one of us."

# You are of the LIGHT

Within everyone there is the

# LIGHT

We call it our Essence or Spirit.

It is eternal.

It is our

# BEST SELF.

It leads us to wholeness, peace, joy and right action.

## Some qualities of Your Essence/Spirit

Circle the ones that describe your Spirit

| | | | | |
|---|---|---|---|---|
| Caring | Kind | Loving | Thoughtful | Alive |
| Curious | Courageous | Strong | Calm | |
| Patient | Sharing | Real/No Pretending | Clear | |
| Just ME | Creative | Trusting | Open | |
| Centered | Accepting | Loving | Forgiving | |
| Compassionate | Peaceful | Confident | Lovable | |
| Wise | My Best Self | Self-Directed | Just Knows | |
| Grounded | Intuitive | Connected | Honest | |

# Draw a picture of your BEST SELF

And/or list other qualities not listed on pg 34

# VALIDATE And CELEBRATE YOUR GIFTS !

Your body thrives when you validate and celebrate YOU and YOUR GIFTS.

# Things I like about Myself:

Be sure to include your talents and gifts ♡

## Who I Am

It is a gift you give your self to keep a growing list of things you like about your self and that others like about you.

People will come and go in your life and many will tell you what they like about you.

It's good to write it down so when you need a reminder of who you are you can read your lists and let the words fall in.

This is called <u>Validation.</u>

# What others like about me:

Read the lists you just wrote out loud

see pages 37 & 39

Allow the positive energy to fill your body as you read the things you like about your self
and
the things others like about you.

Notice how it feels to say these out loud.

Validation is a loving practice for yourself and everyone in your life!

Now practice Validating others.

Tell them what you like about them.

Validation nourishes
our wholeness
and
our knowing

When Something Inside You

Just Knows...

This is Your

Intuition

Your

Inner Wisdom

Your Mind Knows Things

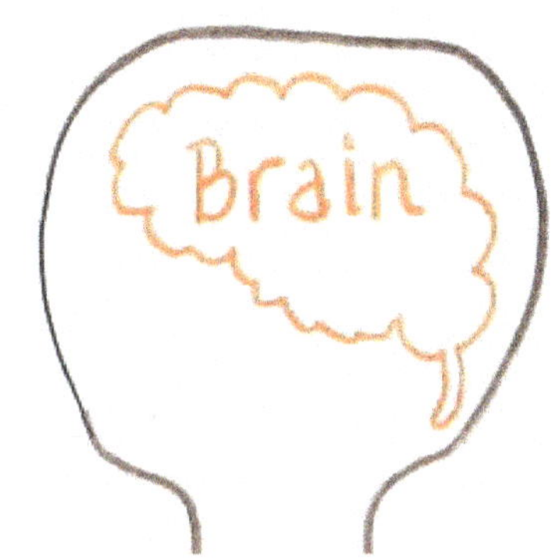


Your Heart Has Wisdom

Your Gut Feelings Give Answers

LISTENING to your self is important.

When you listen to your self you learn to trust what you know to be true about you and your experience.

One way we learn to listen to ourselves is to be still and get centered.

This is often called Meditation.

Some call it a Centering Practice.

# Centering Practice/Meditation:

Stand or sit still.

Feel your Length.

(reach up with your head to the stars/extend down into the earth)

Feel your Width. (sense your sides from head/ears and hips)

Feel your Depth. (feel your front and your back of body)

Breathe in and out.

Feel your whole body become present.

Notice what you're feeling inside.

Listen as you allow your body to speak.

♥ Having a centering/stillness practice and asking for inner guidance will help keep you connected to your vision/purpose.

You can use this centering practice before a presentation/speech or important conversation to bring yourself most present and ready.

You can ask your whole self
anything you want to know.

You might ask what your body needs
to heal if you're sick.

You can ask where to look for
your next career opportunity.

You can ask for what to say
in a difficult conversation you need to have.

You can find peace in the stillness.

When I listen to my heart♡

I will know my truth
and the right actions to take

I will know Who I AM

and what my purpose is for being

and what gifts I have to share
with the world.

"Your vision
will become clear
only when you can look
into your own heart.

Those who look outside,
dream;

Those who look inside;
awaken!"

~Carl Jung

# Follow Your Inner Guidance

If you follow someone else's compass

it will take you somewhere

other than where you

were meant to go.

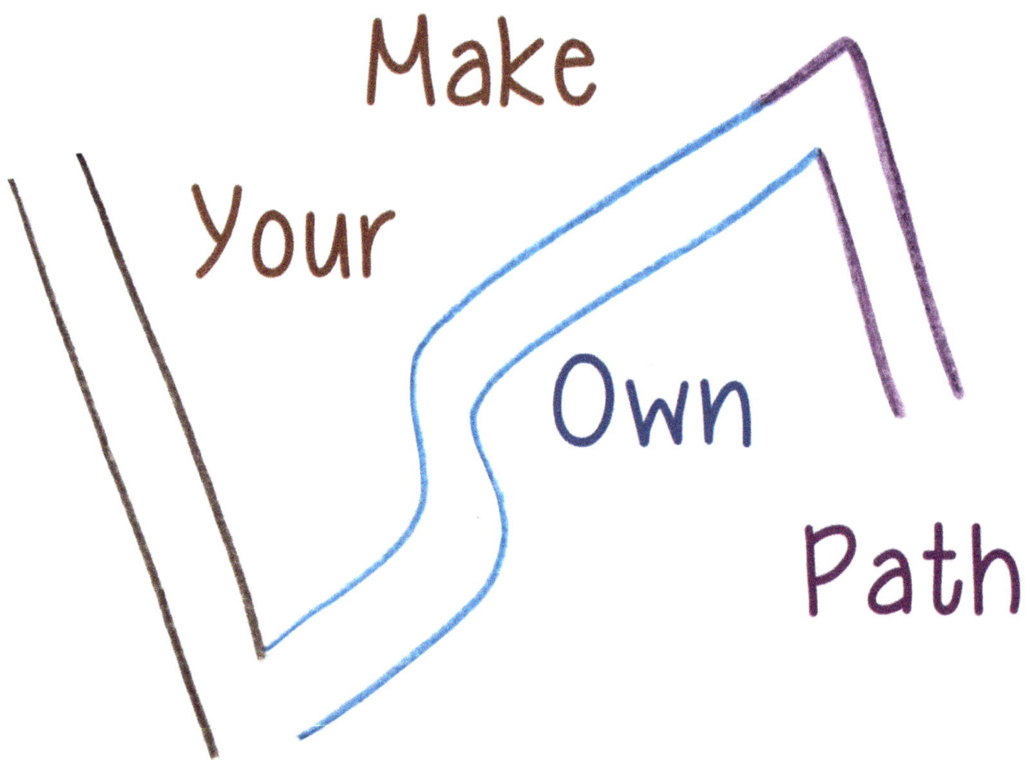

There is NO ONE else exactly like YOU.

Every human being is a unique individual.

No one has the same fingerprint.

And just like snowflakes,

Be
Who You Are
and
Reach for
the Stars

# DISCOVER YOUR PASSIONS

When you do

what you LOVE

you feel good inside.

These are

your PASSIONS.

# Circle the things you love to DO:

Soccer Baseball Hiking Reading

Study/Research Running Bicycling Camping

Writing Basketball Swimming Piano

Guitar Drums Be with animals Seeing Friends

Tennis Bowling Canoeing Painting Science

Making Music Cooking/Baking Making Things

Arts/Crafts Surfing Dancing Fishing

Driving Snowboarding Skating Skiing

Sailing Drawing Star Gazing Carving Wood

Building Things Gardening Learning Traveling

## These Are Your Passions.

# Your Passions Are Like Branches of Your Tree

## Sample of a Passion Tree

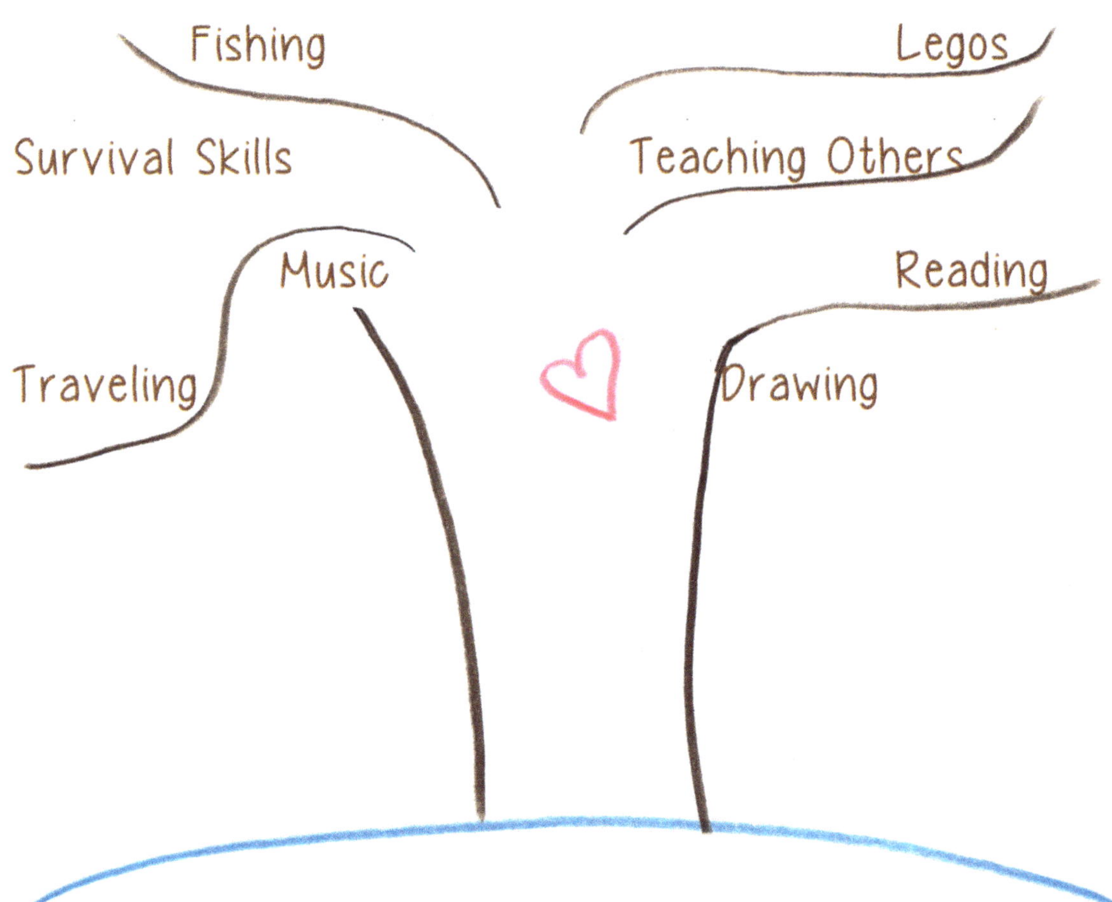


What you love to do expands your gifts out into the world.

# Draw your Passion Tree

You may have many branches of passions or you may have a few branches of things you love to do.

Remember each one of us is unique
so your passion tree will be
different than others'.

The adventure of a life is enriched when
you grow into your favorite passions,
and yet you can try on new ones.

You can reach and "branch" out toward
the passions and gifts you want to
experience and express more fully.

When people do their passions they feel:

HAPPY

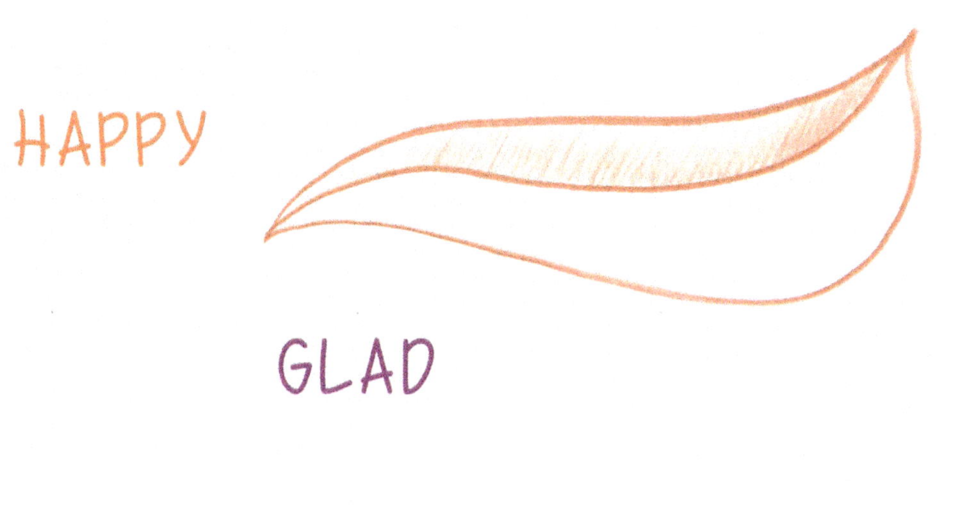

GLAD

EXCITED

ALIVE

What else do you feel inside your body when you are doing your passions?

When you do what you love you can feel light, tingly, peaceful, relaxed and time goes by quickly.

This is called "being in the FLOW."

Choosing to do what we love gives us energy, ease, joy and more fulfillment.

These are called SENSATIONS.

You feel sensations within your body.

Sometimes they feel good,
sometimes they feel neutral
and sometimes they feel uncomfortable.

When you follow your good sensations
you know you love what you are doing.

As you grow and do what you love your
branches grow into areas where your energy
leads you and you want to do more of it.

Sensations are another key guide
for your journey.

Think of a time you were doing something new.

Remember how your body felt inside.

Did you feel sweaty, tingly, numb, cold, hot or was your heart thumping?

When you do something new it can sometimes feel uncomfortable at first.

These SENSATIONS inform us of what is going on inside us at that moment.

It is energy that moves in and out of us.

# More Sensations

Tingly Shaky Scared Dry

Butterflies in stomach Light Tense

Relieved Hot Cold Hopeful

Tickled Safe Cozy Numb

Strong Hungry Tired Itchy

Excited Relaxed Warm Sexy

Sometimes your sensations tell you to

MOVE AWAY

from something or someone.

<u>This is important information.</u>

Please listen to your body.

<u>Your body doesn't lie.</u>

Your body will tell you if you need to set a boundary and say "NO" to whatever or whoever is not good for you.

Having a healthy NO is very important.

## Practice saying NO.

You decide WHO you want to invite into your circle of life.

You decide what you allow into your body and mind.

Choose by listening to your body sensations.

# Boundary Setting Practice

## The Rope Circle

Take a rope or string and make a circle around you on the floor. You are in the middle of the circle. The area between you and the rope circle is your personal space. You're in the center. You can make your circle as big as you like.

Imagine someone wants to enter into your circle. You can practice saying "No," "Not now" or "Yes, come into my circle."

Your circle may be small some days or larger on other days. You may want a few people near or many people close to you.

You have permission to practice sensing when you want to say NO and use your voice to express your truth of how you feel at that time.

# Rope Circle

"When you have
a healthy
NO

You will have
a healthy
YES."

- Pam McLean, Hudson Institute

Remember to listen
to your
body's sensations
and trust
your intuition.

They will guide you
throughout your life.

# It is Natural to Feel All of My Feelings

# Emotions Are Like Leaves.

Emotions are energy.

Emotions move and change.

Emotions are Messengers.

Emotions give me important information.

I can have many feelings at once.

All of my feelings are a natural part of being human.

Sometimes I feel happy

Sometimes I feel sad

Sometimes I feel silly

Sometimes I feel afraid

Sometimes I feel excited

Sometimes I feel angry

## Emotions are Messengers.

When you feel angry it is letting you know that something just happened that is NOT OK! And you might be feeling hurt.

Think about the last time you were angry.

Remember what happened that wasn't OK.

Anger is just like all emotions. It is ENERGY that needs to move out of you and it is telling you how you feel about something that has happened.

Releasing your feelings is an important practice so you can be healthy and peaceful.

## Healthy ways to release feelings:

When you are sad crying can help release the pain.

When you are angry you can express and release anger/frustration in various ways:

You can talk to someone about it.

You can hit a foam bat on a pillow to vent the frustration and anger safely without hurting anyone (especially your self).

You can write an anger letter and tear it up.

Letting my feelings flow
is important because

feelings that get stuck inside
can make me sick.

Scientists have discovered that tears help to release from our body a stress hormone (called Cortisol) which means crying is key to staying healthy and reducing aggression.

My body needs to express
what I am feeling

and

My body is designed
to release all of my emotions naturally.

Crying is good for ME

and everyone else.

So is Laughing Ourselves Silly

I'm going to let all of my feelings flow

# Circle the feelings you have felt before:

Abandoned
Accepted
Afraid
Accused
Agitated
Alone
Angry
Annoyed
Anxious
Bullied
Belittled
Betrayed
Bored
Capable

Cautious
Confident
Confused
Courageous
Criticized
Crushed
Defeated
Delighted
Disappointed
Disconnected
Discouraged
Distracted
Disrespected
Dread

Excited
Fearful
Frightened
Frustrated
Funny
Grateful
Guilty
Happy
Heart broken
Helpless
Hopeful
Humiliated
Hurt
Hyper

Ignored

Important

Insecure

Intimidated

Invisible

Irritated

Jealous

Left out

Let down

Lonely

Lost

Loved ♡

Manipulated

Misunderstood

Moody

Needed

Neglected

Nervous

Not believed

Not heard

Not trusted

Numb

Overwhelmed

Peaceful

Picked on

Proud

Pressured

Protective

Quiet

Resentful

Rejected

Rushed

Sad

Scared

Shy

Silly

Stuck

Stressed

Self-Conscious

Tense

Ticked Off

Tired

Trapped

Uninterested

Worried

Your Feelings often give you clues to what you really need.

<u>List the things you need right now:</u>

Communicating
My Needs
In A Kind
Clear Way
Is A Practice

## Naming my NEEDS and making REQUESTS

One way to communicate my needs clearly and kindly is to say:

"Would you be willing to...?"

If they say "no" you could then say

"When would you be willing to...?"

They will likely negotiate a time
to give you what you are requesting.

If you can wait for that time period
then all is well.

However, if they say "later" or "not ever"
then you can express your specific need.

"I understand you don't want to
but I need to... because..."

<u>This is Non-Violent Communication.</u>

When we use language like

"Are you willing?"

We invite others to hear our request and not feel that we are being demanding.

"I am feeling…"

"I need…"

"I would like to spend time with you."

"Would you be willing to help me with this now?"

Listening to others

and

allowing them to

communicate their needs

is important, too.

This is how you can learn

to understand

and see where they are coming from

and what is true for them.

Be Curious!

When people have asked you,

"What do you want to be?"

Have you ever said...

"The Best ME
I Can Be!"

My Future = Who I Want to Be

"The two most important days are...

The day you were born

and

The day you find out

WHY

YOU were born"

~Mark Twain

Honor Your
Hopes
And
Your Dreams

"Dream no small dream
for they have no power to move
the hearts of men."

~ Goethe

"The future belongs to those who believe
in the beauty of their dreams."

~ Eleanor Roosevelt

"Some men see things
as they are
and ask why?

Others dream things
that never were
and ask why not?"

~ George Bernard Shaw

Having dreams
is part of living whole.

Your dreams often reveal
what you truly want.

# I dream about:

"Your imagination is a preview of life's coming attractions."

- Albert Einstein

When you believe...

Magic can happen.

# If You Believe

Download song at www.GrowingUpWhole.com

If you believe, within your heart you'll know
That no one can change, the path that you must go
Believe that you can go home, believe you can float on air
Then click your heels 3 times, If you believe, then you'll be there
Believe in your Self right from the start
Believe in the magic that's inside your heart
Believe all these things not because I told you to
But believe in your Self, just believe in your Self
Just believe in your Self as I believe in you
Believe there's a reason to be
Believe you can float on air
And know from the moment you try
If you believe, then you'll be there
Believe in your Self, right from the start
And you'll have a brain and you'll have a heart
And you'll have the courage to last your whole life through
But believe in your Self, If you believe in your Self
Just believe in your Self, as I believe in You!

Written by C. Smalls from the musical "The Wiz"

"Go confidently
in the direction
of your dreams.

Live the life
you have imagined."

~ Harry David Thoreau

# VISIONING as a Practice

Visioning helps create your life the way you want it to be.

Imagine how you want your day to go.

See your self moving through the day exactly as you desire it to be.

Feel the sensations of how it will feel.

Choose this vision for your self.

## Visioning can be used in all areas of life.

Visualize making the points in the meeting.

Visualize playing well.

Visualize the conversation going as you desire.

Visualize your body healing any illness you have.

# Make a Vision Board

Putting your vision onto paper is called a Vision Board.

You can take magazine pictures you cut out or words or draw/paint your own images on a big poster board.

Paste or draw/paint your vision just as you want it.

An example:

If you wanted to go to Italy and spend your birthday with a particular person you would cut out pictures of places and experiences you want to have in Italy with them and paste them on the board.

It becomes a visual reminder of your heart's desires.

You can put anything on it. (health, work, travel, peace, love, friends, the home you wish to live in)

Watch and see how your visions come true.

# My Vision:

# Let Your Heart

Making lists and/or drawing pictures of what you wish for helps you stay connected to what you truly want

and connected to all POSSIBILITIES

of having what you want.

IT's FUN to wish for anything

and everything

your heart desires. ♡

You may not always get everything

you wish for,

but having wishes, hopes and dreams

makes life more fun and magical.

# Make WISH LISTS

You can make them anytime of the year...

## What I want for my next BIRTHDAY! 

Make a list or draw pictures of what you are wishing for:

## What I want for the HOLIDAYS!

### Make a list or draw pictures of what you want

Include: Gifts and Feelings and Experiences you want to have:

## What I wish for the world and others to have:

# Treasure Your IMAGINATION

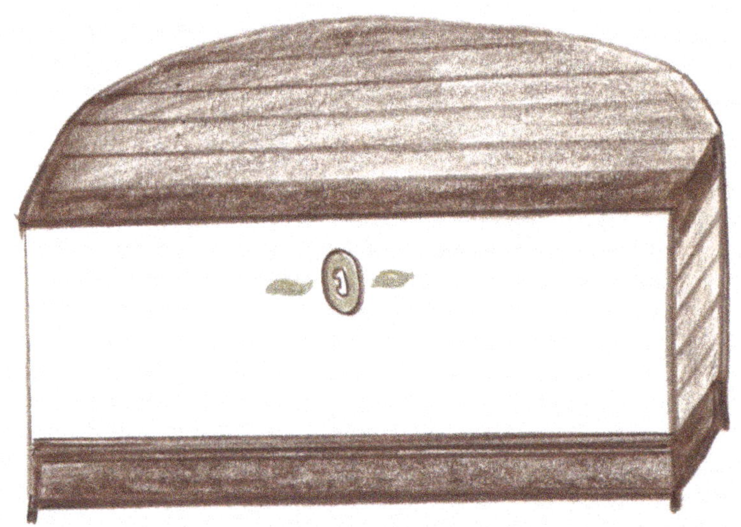

"If you can imagine it,
you can achieve it.

If you can dream it,
you can become it."

~ William Arthur Ward

Honor

and cherish

your

CREATIVITY

## Circle the ways you like to create:

Drawing Painting Clay/Ceramics Wood working

Crocheting Needlework Weaving Knitting

Carving Building Cooking Fixing Cars

Sewing Writing Stories Songwriting Baking/Cooking

Playing instruments/making music Software Design

Tying Flies Making up games Origami

Add any of your creative activities not listed here:

"I am not afraid of storms,
for I am learning
how to sail
my ship."

~ Louise May Alcott "Little Women"

# When Storms Come

## My Boat Will Be Ready

# Navigate Life
# with
# Resilience
# and
# Positive Life Skills

Keep believing in your self.

Especially when things are hard.

Sometimes bad things will happen
and you will get hurt.

Sometimes you won't get what you
wish for.

Sometimes you will lose.

Sometimes you will fall off.

Sometimes you will make mistakes.

Hard things will happen.

There will be loss and grief.

Sometimes people will mistreat you and be mean.

But what is AMAZING is that you will...

B O U N C E

BACK

Yes

You

Will

Bounce Back!

Because

YOU are BIGGER

than

ANYTHING

That has ever happened to you

and

YOU are RESILIENT!

"You're braver

than you believe ♡

Stronger than you know

and

Smarter than you think."

~ A.A. Milne "Winnie the Pooh"

When you're feeling down you can bounce back by doing some of these things:

Go out in nature. Take a walk. Connect with the earth.

Draw/Paint/Make something/Express your creativity.

Play or listen to music you like.

Hang out with animals.

Talk to a loving friend or family member.

Volunteer to help others/Give back.

Other things that can help when you are feeling down:

Feel and release all of your emotions.

Have a good cry.

Howl at the moon. ☺ Dance.

Write in a Journal.

Remember the truth of who you are.

Remember a time you felt happy before

and

Remind your self "I CAN DO THIS!"

When you say "I CAN"... You CAN.

Try it!

Next time you are doing something new
or something that feels hard

Say to your self
"I CAN"

"The moment you doubt whether you can fly,
you cease forever being able to do it."

~ Peter Pan

## What I Say Matters.

The power of my words can make more things possible.

EnCOURAGing words helps us all find our COURAGE.

"I am learning here,
I am not failing."

~ Johnny

# Persistence Pays

## Never Give Up

Remember that Thomas Edison
made 1,000 light bulbs
before he got one that worked
the way he hoped it could.

What if he had stopped at # 394 ?

You may have some very challenging things to deal with.

Remember your spirit and body are

STRONG

and you can use all your skills, talents, tools, practices, and resilience to get through anything and accomplish all that you dream of.

Remember the first time you did something really scary and you did it anyway.

Inside you

is a very

BRAVE and

COURAGEOUS Person

Who has already done

amazing things.

Validate your courageous Acts.

## Courageous things I've done in my life:

Remember You

can do anything!

WORDS

can heal

and

change the world.

Practice using positive words
that make you and others feel good.

## What are your favorite positive words?

Circle the ones you love to hear

You did it I love you Fantastic job

Yes you can You are cool

Wonderful performance You worked hard

You can do it I believe in you Well done

You've got this Beautiful creation

You're smart I like having you as my friend

That was epic Nice catch Love your work

Remember how good it feels when someone says

"THANK YOU."

Remember when someone asks

"PLEASE may I...?"

Remember when someone tells you they

"LOVE YOU and

how happy they are that you were born."

Remember how it feels when someone says,

"WELL DONE! or YOU'VE GOT THIS!"

When you use positive, encouraging words to your self and with your friends amazing things can happen.

Say nice things to

your family/friends/co-workers this week.

Notice how it feels inside you to give positive reinforcement in this way.

Notice what good feelings
the other person
feels when you use positive words.

# Self Loving Practices

## A Self-loving Validation Ritual

Share out loud or write down things you did well lately:

Notice how good it feels to honor your self in this way

Do it every day if you can.

## Creating More Happiness

You can create happiness within by letting the energy of Self-loving validation soak into your whole body.

When someone gives you a compliment, let it land inside you and fill you up with positive feelings.

When you want to feel good remember what it feels like to be loved and cared about.

Allow those wonderful feelings to SOAK IN to every cell in your body. This is called SAVORING the good feelings.

Scientists call this Installing Happiness.

Our brain wires happiness when it feels positive feelings, so celebrate, validate and do things that make you feel happy.

## Celebrate

## The JOY of Life!

List all the ways you love to celebrate:

Self validation builds your resilience.

Other things that help you feel happy, bounce back and stay balanced are

Compassion and Gratitude.

COMPASSION is:

The desire to remove pain and suffering.

Compassion is when your heart feels for someone else's pain and you wish their pain would stop.

You can also have compassion for your self.

When you are hurting you can feel your heart wishing that your own pain would stop.

GRATITUDE is:

Feeling appreciation in your heart and saying "Thank You" and/or writing thank you notes.

WHAT are you thankful for?

"No act
of kindness,
no matter how small,
is ever wasted."

~ Aesop's Fables

The Lion and the Mouse

# WHO are you thankful for?

Write some thank you notes or say thank you to these people above and tell them how much you value their steadfast loving support.

# My Actions
# Affect Other People.

The Golden Rule reminds us to:

**Treat others the way**
**we would like to be treated.**

And yet sometimes
people do not act kindly.

Sometimes people will say or do things that hurt you.

They might do this if they are feeling hurt, stressed, tired or angry.

It helps to practice letting these things fly past you and not let them land in your heart (if possible).

However, sometimes hurtful words and actions do land inside us.

You can release this negative energy.

## Energy Release Practice:

When someone's energy or words hurt you you can SHAKE THEM OFF.

Yes, your body can SHAKE, SHIVER, SQUIRM and DANCE as you WIGGLE and GIGGLE your way free of the icky, sticky sensations.

Try it!

Imagine someone has just said or done something that hurts.

Now imagine it's a color or a shape of something sticky.

Let your body shake it off,
squirm and wiggle
and toss it off of you.

Have fun!

When you're all done notice how it feels to be free of that negative energy.

FEEL your good feelings
and reinstall happiness.

You can shake off anything

and then...

It's a good time to practice COMPASSION for someone else who may be hurting and wish that their pain would stop.

People can hurt others or put their energy on to others when they are hurting.

It's NOT OK but it happens.

Picture their heart and your heart healing and becoming peaceful once the pain stops.

Forgiveness is a gift I give
to myself and to others.

We all can say or do things that hurt
others sometimes.

Practice saying "I forgive you"

and

"Please forgive me."

Asking for and giving forgiveness is a precious gift we give each other and to the world.

When we let go of past hurts we create
peace and a space for good things
to enter into all our lives.

We create freedom for all human beings
to be their best selves and shine
their light in the world.

This is what the world needs;

all people living as their Best Self,

sharing their gifts and making the world
a better more peaceful loving place.

I Forgive Myself for:

I Forgive Others for:

It is a Gift I give to myself

and to the world

To Own my Wholeness

And BE ME

Shining My Unique Light

in the World!

# This Little Light of Mine

Download song at www.GrowingUpWhole.com

This little light of mine, I'm gonna let it shine

This little light of mine, I'm gonna let it shine
This little light of mine, I'm gonna let it shine
Let it shine, let it shine, let it shine

With my heart and soul, I'm gonna let it shine

With my heart and soul, I'm gonna let it shine
With my heart and soul, I'm gonna let it shine
Let it shine, let it shine, let it shine

Everywhere I go, I'm gonna let it shine

Everywhere I go, I'm gonna let it shine
Everywhere I go, I'm gonna let it shine
Let it shine, let it shine, let it shine

Won't let anyone blow it out, I'm gonna let it shine

Won't let anyone blow it out, I'm gonna let it shine
Won't let anyone blow it out, I'm gonna let it shine
Let it shine, let it shine, let it shine

Public Domain – Linda Newlin Arrangement on Cd Love Your Self

Reminders
For
My
Journey

It is natural to SHINE MY LIGHT IN THE WORLD.

I am whole and I am complete just as I am now.

Feeling my feelings will help me stay connected to my wholeness, the earth and all living things. I will be healthy, balanced, ☮ peaceful and connected.

I am a part of everything.

I stay balanced, healthy and resilient through life's ups and downs by using my self-loving practices (validation, feeling my feelings, compassion, giving and receiving forgiveness and cherishing my hopes, dreams and wishes).

My Inner Guidance will take me where my heart wants to be. ♡

Finding MY life's purpose and sharing my gifts will bring the greatest joy.

I will BELIEVE in my self and say "I CAN".

It is my birthright to claim my place on the earth and to grow deep roots, a strong heart, expansive branches and feel the feelings that come and go with living.

I Will Dream Big!

Say "YES" to You!

Yes to your hopes, dreams and wishes!

Yes to Living Whole and Being YOU!

Yes to protecting your earth home!

Yes to World Peace!

Yes to everyone being their Best Self!

Your heart
is big enough

for every one
and every thing.

We're all part of a circle of life here on earth.

There are billions of people on the planet and each one is unique and brings their own special gifts.

YOU are unique and so is everyone else.

Celebrate The Gift of Living Whole.

Thank you for cherishing all beings and taking care of the earth.

We dream of a world where all people grow up knowing who they are and cherishing their gifts and talents,

growing into all areas of their passions,

bouncing back from life's hard moments,

and knowing they are love, loving and lovable

at all times.

Peace to You on Your Journey. Linda ☮

This book is dedicated to all my
teachers, coaches and healers
who helped me find my wholeness and reclaim the courage
to shine my Light in the World!

Thank you! ♡

Inspirational gifts and articles available at

GrowingUpWhole.com

Validation Journals

Music and More

Growing Up Whole: A Child's Guide Book

Being Whole: A Teen's Guide Book

Raising Whole Children: A Parent's Guide Book (coming fall 2015)

♥a portion of all profits go to children who are healing from trauma

Living Whole
A Guide Book
Linda Newlin

www.ingramcontent.com/pod-product-compliance
Lightning Source LLC
Chambersburg PA
CBHW051611030426
42334CB00035B/3487

* 9 7 8 0 9 9 6 2 0 6 5 0 1 *